TEEN
ISSUES

Conflict Resolution
The Win-Win Situation

Carolyn Casey

Enslow Publishers, Inc.

40 Industrial Road	PO Box 38
Box 398	Aldershot
Berkeley Heights, NJ 07922	Hants GU12 6BP
USA	UK

http://www.enslow.com

Library of Congress Cataloging-in-Publication data

Casey, Carolyn.
　　Conflict resolution : the win-win situation / by Carolyn Casey.
　　　　p. cm. — (Teen issues)
　　Includes bibliographical references and index.
　　Contents: Conflict resolution : finding solutions without giving up or giving in —
Teenagers have a steady diet of conflict — Conflict resolution : being powerful
without fighting — Fight or flight? finding a middle ground — Roadblocks to
success – Using conflict resolution skills in the community.
　　ISBN 0-7660-1584-X
　　1. Interpersonal conflict in adolescence—Juvenile literature. 2. Conflict
management—Juvenile literature. [1. Conflict management. 2. Interpersonal
relations.). I. Title. II. Series.

BF724.3 .I56 C37　2001
303.6'9—dc21
　　　　　　　　　　　　　　　　　　　　　　　00-009786
　　　　　　　　　　　　　　　　　　　　　　　CIP

Printed in the United States of America

10 9 8 7 6 5 4 3 2 1

To Our Readers:
All Internet addresses in this book were active and appropriate when we went to press.
Any comments or suggestions can be sent by e-mail to Comments@enslow.com or to the
address on the back cover.

Illustration credits: Courtesy of Carolyn Casey, pp. 19, 23, 37, 39, 48, 51;
Diamar, p. 16; Skjold, pp. 8, 27, 43.

Cover Illustration: Portrait by Ed French; Background © Corel Corporation.

Contents

1

Finding Solutions Without Giving Up or Giving In

If peoples' just grievances are constantly denied and ignored, sooner or later their anger boils over into violence. We all know that.

—Kofi Annan, secretary general of the United Nations at the Hague Appeal for Peace Conference, 1999[1]

Turn on the television at five o'clock and the newscasters describe the latest wars in foreign countries, the shooting between two teen street gangs, and a human interest story about a custody battle between two parents.

While each news story is different, all of them are about conflict.

Now think about the latest conversations heard in the hallway between classes. One girl accuses another girl of stealing her jacket. Two guys accidentally bump shoulders and square off as if to start a fight. And, of course, there are

Conflict: (noun) 1. A fight or struggle, especially a prolonged one; battle; 2. A disagreement, dispute, or quarrel; 3. A mental or spiritual struggle within a person; 4. The clashing of opposed principles or statements.

always a few people complaining about how unfairly their parents are acting.

Although these conversations might not be as dramatic as warfare or shootings, they also are about people experiencing conflicts.

For as long as there have been people, there have been conflicts. In fact, conflicts may have existed before there were people, since conflicts even show up among animals. Watch two dogs as they try to establish territory, determine who owns a bone, or compete for a Frisbee flying through the air. Each tree they mark or bone they chew is a potential conflict. They may resolve it peaceably and agree on territory, they might have a standoff and pose snarling, or they could wind up in a dogfight with the fur flying.

People are not much different, except there usually is not any fur flying.

Every day people deal with large or small conflicts. And every day people make choices that can make those conflicts—or disagreements—get solved or get worse. Of course, people have more choices than animals. One of those choices can be learning the skills to resolve conflicts without giving up or giving in.

Although everyone experiences conflict, it is most common during the teenage years. Many teens feel as if their days are filled with arguments with parents and teachers and misunderstandings with friends. At times, teens even feel in conflict with themselves as they develop their values and beliefs.

Increasing Violence Alarms the Nation

For generations, people just accepted the idea that teenagers would have a steady dose of conflict in their lives at home and at school. Physical fights between youth were considered a normal part of growing up. And even though gang rumbles were discouraged by police, they rarely ended in major shoot-outs.

But in the 1990s, more and more schools experienced the dangers of students bringing weapons to school. A number of tragedies occurred when those weapons were used to kill people.

Between July 1994 and June 1998, there were 173 reported major incidents of school violence. The majority of these were homicides and involved the use of guns. A federal study in 1997 reported that 18.3 percent of high school students carried a weapon within thirty days of being surveyed.[2]

People around the country were shocked in 1998 when high school student Kip Kinkel walked into Thurston High School in Springfield, Oregon, and fired fifty rounds from a .22-caliber semiautomatic rifle, killing two students and wounding twenty-five others. Before that, in Jonesboro, Arkansas, two middle school boys, Andrew Golden and Mitchell Johnson, shot and killed four students and a teacher at Westside Middle School.

Cases of students shooting their classmates and teachers at school are uncommon and most students will never experience this extreme of violence. But they are faced with the reality that more weapons are coming to school, which increases the chances that a disagreement could turn deadly.

Almost two hundred incidents of school violence that occurred in a four-year period involved the use of guns.

A schoolyard fight that might have ended with bumps and bruises in the 1970s could end in knifings or gunshots today.

In 1998, after the shootings at Thurston High School in Oregon, President Bill Clinton ordered the Department of Education and the Department of Justice to help find ways to stop these crimes. The two agencies wrote reports with ideas about dealing with violent students and teaching conflict resolution skills. In their report, "Early Warning/ Timely Response: A Guide to Safe Schools," their conclusion was that teaching students effective ways to deal with disagreements was essential. They also developed information to help teachers, parents, and students recognize and protect themselves from teens who were dangerously angry.[3]

Punishing adults and teens who commit acts of violence is one solution. But most people believe it is better to stop the violence before it occurs.

One study showed that 14.8 percent of students nationwide had been in a physical fight on school property one or more times in the past year. Overall, male students (20 percent) were significantly more likely to have a physical fight on school property than female students (8.6 percent).[4]

More and more government leaders are urging people to work on preventing violence. As an example, a few days after Kip Kinkel killed his classmates, Governor John Kitzhaber of Oregon commented, "If you look at the priorities that this state and many other states have reflected over the last four years, the priority has been to build prison cells after crimes have been committed, after victims have been created. I believe this society owes it to itself, to its children, and to its future to make a commitment to prevention that is equally as serious as the commitment we have made to incarceration."[5]

A growing number of schools are teaching students about peaceful ways to resolve conflict. Techniques that once were used only in the business world and in political struggles have been redesigned so they can be used in high schools, middle schools, and even elementary schools.

Kindergarten students are being taught ways to control their anger, deal with the issues, and solve problems. Now, the majority of all public schools include conflict resolution as part of their curriculums. Conflict resolution classes

Resolution: (noun) The act or result of solving. A solution.

show students of all ages how to settle disputes. Students are trained to mediate other people's disagreements and shown ways to control their tempers. Many programs also include ways to recognize dangerously angry people and identify conflict situations that require adult or police intervention.

The History of Conflict Resolution

People have always worked to resolve conflicts. But the field of conflict resolution emerged about eighty years ago as a way to improve labor-management relations. In the 1920s, labor negotiator Mary Parker Follett showed that many conflicts could be solved in ways that benefited everyone. This could be done, she said, if the parties that were arguing stopped bickering over positions and focused on ways to meet their underlying needs.[6] Her approach was for people to seek a "win-win" solution in which both parties in a dispute find a middle ground or a solution that lets them both benefit.

Those early techniques, combined with many others, have transformed conflict resolution into a subject that is taught in most schools. Some colleges even offer degrees in the growing field of conflict resolution.

Former President Jimmy Carter spends a great deal of his time working as a mediator trying to arrange peace agreements for other countries. The techniques he uses are basically the same as those taught in high schools and junior highs around the country.[7]

Students who learn how to use conflict resolution skills to resolve disagreements can use these skills at school, at home, and into adulthood. The techniques explained in this book can be used to deal with disagreements with friends, fights with parents, and even in ongoing battles with brothers and sisters.

A psychologist at the University of Washington studied more than two thousand married couples over twenty-two years and determined that the ability to resolve conflicts was the single most important factor in whether or not each marriage succeeded.[8]

Learning how to resolve conflicts in a way that benefits both people means making sure a disagreement ends without winners and losers. Right now about half of all marriages end in divorce. Perhaps the conflict resolution training being taught to this generation of students may change that figure.

Anyone who is alive experiences conflict. And conflict is not necessarily a bad thing. Conflict can force people to examine their beliefs and goals. It also can help push people toward making changes. The most important thing about conflict is learning how to deal with it effectively in life since everyone faces some amount of conflict every day.

2

Teenagers Have a Steady Diet of Conflict

"I don't have to take this abuse from you. I've got hundreds of other people dying to abuse me."

—Ghostbusters

"Ah, man! I'm only ten and I already have two mortal enemies."

— Bart Simpson from *The Simpsons*

Why Is It So Hard to Be a Teenager?

Brittany stayed up until midnight finishing an overdue social studies project. As she changed into some sweats and climbed into bed, she turned off her alarm clock. Just an extra hour of sleep and I will be fine, she thought as she switched off her lamp. She decided she would do her morning jobs after school. Everyone else in the house was asleep already, so she did not think of asking her mom or stepdad if either one cared when she did her chores.

But the next morning she woke up even later than she had planned. Before her feet hit the floor, her bedroom door flew open and her mom stood there looking mad.

"What are you doing lying around in bed on a school day?" she said, and without waiting for an answer, her mom continued, "I can guarantee that by the time you unload the dishwasher and feed the animals, you'll have missed the bus! I can't believe you haven't even bothered to get dressed."

Just seconds earlier, she felt like everything was under control. She had finished her project and she knew when she would get her jobs done. But now all she felt was angry.

She steamed while she threw on some clothes and stomped through her chores. She did not even bother to tell her mom about her plan to do the work after school. It would just make things worse, she thought. No one around here cares what I think anyway.

Brittany finished putting the last dish away just in time to hear the bus leave without her. That is when her stepdad decided to get involved.

As they got into the car, her stepdad yelled about how irresponsible she always was. She shouted back that she did not like living with him at all. Instead of taking her to school, he dropped her off at the city bus stop where she waited for half an hour before a bus came. Two transfers later, she was finally at school. Social studies was over before she got finished taking her late slip to the office.

She spent the rest of the day inside a storm cloud and managed to get into arguments with her two best friends over things she usually could have ignored. As soon as she got home, she yelled at her brother for going into her room.

By the time she finished her homework, she felt as if she were at war with everyone and thought no one cared what she thought about anything. She went to bed and tossed and turned wondering why her day had been so horrible.[1]

Teen Physical and Mental Development Create Conflict

People experience conflict at every age. But teens have an especially bumpy road. Some days it feels as if everything is going wrong. Often change, even good change, comes with big or small amounts of conflict. And the teen years are filled with changes. It may help to remember that being a teenager often means being in conflict. It may help even more to remember that no one is a teenager forever, just for a few years. During those years, there are a lot of things teenagers can do to make this time period easier. Just realizing that changes in their bodies might make teens more anxious or upset can help them not overreact to small problems. This is also the perfect time to learn new skills for communication and conflict resolution so that teens can deal directly with their problems. Keeping a journal or talking with a close friend can be especially helpful ways to sort out emotions and problems.

Mood Swings

The human body creates many hormones that are linked to the rapid physical growth and the sexual development that occur in the teen years. Changes in the amount of hormones the body is producing or girls' monthly hormone fluctuations from menstruating can make teens feel moody, tense, or depressed. Hormones are chemical substances that travel through the bloodstream. Testosterone is the main male hormone and estrogen and progesterone are the

Writing feelings down in a journal is a great way of letting emotions out.

primary female hormones. Both males and females will attain their adult height, weight, musculoskeletal, and organ size between the ages of thirteen and twenty.[2] These rapid physical changes can cause conflict because of mood swings and general discomfort with new body shapes.

Pushing for Independence

During the teenage years, people begin developing their own beliefs and values. Certainly, the values and beliefs their families taught them are important, but teens begin really looking at them and deciding which ones fit. And that can lead to a lot of conflict, both inside the teenager and within the family.

In *Making Sense of Your Teenager*, psychologist Lawrence Kutner writes,

> A teenager's natural drive toward independence is sometimes in conflict with a parent's hope for family harmony. A teenager's desire to explore more complex and abstract issues—to exercise and test the developing areas of his brain just as he strengthens and tests his developing muscles—often means that he questions his parents' beliefs about such matters as religion and justice.[3]

While constant battles are the sign of deeper problems, a reasonable amount of parent-teen conflict is not only normal, but helpful as well. One way that teenagers learn who they are is by challenging others who have different beliefs.[4]

At the same time, teenagers are becoming more independent. During middle school or junior high, many teens begin taking on jobs like babysitting or mowing lawns to earn money. They also have more freedom in choosing their clothes, picking out movies, and spending more time alone with friends.

These steps toward independence often involve a tug-of-war between parents and their children. Some of the parent/teen conflict is about balancing the teens' need for independence with the parents' need to supervise and guide them. Some of the conflict comes from a teen pushing parents away, often in anger, to help separate from parents.

Early adolescents (middle school age) often make up reasons to get angry with their parents so they can feel more comfortable about becoming more independent of them.[5]

During the teen years, people grow from being dependent upon their families for guidance, rules, housing, and

A fourteen-year-old girl wants to stay out with her friends until midnight, but her parents set an 11 P.M. curfew. Conflict.

A thirteen-year-old boy's parents say he cannot go hang out at the mall with his friends for three hours. Conflict.

Another set of parents say their teen daughter cannot go to school all dressed in black even though all of her friends are wearing these Gothic style clothes. Conflict.

financial support to being adults, living independently, making their own rules, and working to earn money. That is a lot of change packed into just a few years.

Friendships

Young children usually want their parent's approval and acceptance. They want to follow their parent's values, rules, and even opinions on appropriate clothing to get that approval.

Teens can feel just the opposite. It can be much more important that their friends approve of their clothing or hairstyle. They become more interested in their friends' or peers' values and ideas than in their parents'. This can create external conflict between the teen and parents, the teen and peers, as well as internal conflicts as a teen tries to sort out the values and viewpoints of friends. Peer pressure can leave a teen feeling pushed to do things that conflict with his values or family rules.

This also is the age when teens form small groups, or cliques, that exclude some students because of the way they act or dress.

Media

Television, magazines, movies, and the radio can provide plenty of entertainment. But they can also contribute to conflict for teens determining their values and views.

The media often portray violence as the normal way to settle disagreements. People get shot, beaten up, or killed every night on television. Rarely do the shows portray actors sitting down and working together to resolve a conflict. Popular rap songs are filled with aggression. Yet in real life, people are expected to work out, not shoot out, their problems.

Some of those same conflicts exist within the media's portrayal of sexuality and body image. Women in particular are shown as being beautiful by being very thin. This

When cliques form, certain people end up being excluded simply because of the way they dress or act.

degree of thinness usually can only be achieved through unhealthy dieting. But teens, who are in the middle of a huge growth spurt, are encouraged to eat plenty of nutritious food.

In the movies and on television, actors are shown having sex with people they hardly know. They are rarely shown talking about the risks of pregnancy or sexual diseases. Nor are they often shown talking about whether they should be having sex at all. Meanwhile teens are told to wait until they are older and to only be intimate when they are in a committed relationship and, even then, to take precautions against accidental pregnancy or diseases. It can be difficult for anyone to sort out the mixed messages when parents and teachers tell teenagers one thing yet the media bombards them with opposite messages.

In many ways, the media can add to the inner conflict and pressures faced by teens. When teens are listening to the messages sent by music lyrics or the actions in a movie, they should ask themselves whether what they are seeing or hearing matches their values. If a movie is violent, teenagers can talk to each other about other ways the conflicts could have been handled.

3

Being Powerful Without Fighting

This has been not only a horrible, traumatic experience for you, it's been a traumatic experience for all of America. I am immensely impressed and proud of you for the way you've come back from this and gone on.

—President Bill Clinton, addressing Thurston High School students one month after two students were killed and twenty-five injured in a school shooting.[1]

Working for Solutions

David could not believe it when he opened his report card. He was not surprised by his good grade in math, since that subject always came easily for him. But he could not understand why his English grade was so low. He had finished all of his assignments for that class and gotten acceptable grades on them. And everyone liked his speech about baseball. But there was a C on his report card.

He started feeling really angry with the teacher. Until he opened his report card, he thought he liked the teacher. Now he instantly sided with all the students who sat in the back row of the class and whispered mean comments about Mrs. Angelo.

And he dreaded showing the report card to his parents, who always pushed him to get good grades. By the time he got home, he was furious. He really wanted to confront his teacher. His fists were clenched and his cheeks felt hot.

His anger was clear as he told his parents about the grade. Usually they sided with his teachers. But this time they listened when he explained how unfair he thought the grade was. He wanted to complain about how horrible Mrs. Angelo was. He wanted to describe what a terrible teacher and basically rotten person she was. Instead he stuck to the facts about why he thought the grade was not fair.

Rather than criticizing him for the low grade, David's parents suggested he write a letter to the teacher telling her why he thought he should have gotten a better grade. They refused to call the teacher and argue his case for him, telling him that, at thirteen years old, he could do this on his own.

David struggled with the letter. He tore up several versions. His parents reminded him that it would cause greater problems if he showed his anger or was critical of the teacher in the letter. He asked his parents to read several versions until he was sure he had succeeded in complaining about the grade without attacking the teacher.

His approach helped him. When Mrs. Angelo met with David after she read his letter, she praised him for making some good points. Although she was not willing to change his grade, she promised David that she would consider those points when grading David's work in the future. After a few months had passed, David said he thought he

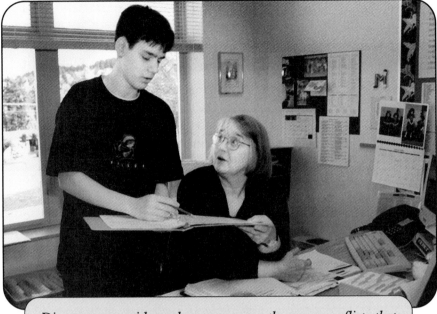

Disagreements with teachers are among the many conflicts that teens may face each day.

was being graded more fairly. He said the hardest part was setting aside his anger and remaining calm in the meeting and in writing his letter. He was able to do this because he practiced telling his side of the story to his parents the night before. Just writing all those angry notes that he tore up helped him get rid of some of his anger.[2]

What Is the Difference Between Arguing and Conflict Resolution?

David understood the difference between arguing and conflict resolution. He knew that if he yelled at his teacher and demanded a higher grade he risked getting into trouble and having worse things appear on his next report card. He accepted that his teacher would not change his grade and saw a compromise in Mrs. Angelo's promise to take his ideas into consideration in future grades. Both teacher and student gained something. There was no one winner.

Researchers at the Institute for Conflict Analysis and Resolution (ICAR) at George Mason University report that conflict is the product of unmet needs and unrecognized differences. The Institute's leaders say that conflict is a normal part of people interacting and is neither good nor bad.[3]

One of the first steps in learning about conflict resolution is understanding the difference between arguing and conflict resolution. Arguing involves people telling their side of the story and fighting (sometimes physically) for what they want. It does not include listening to the other side of the story or looking for any solution other than the one with which they started.

Conflict resolution involves both people in a disagreement agreeing to roll up their sleeves and work together to find a solution. Sometimes a peer or adult mediator helps teens in conflict find a solution. The focus is not on one side winning or on putting someone down. Instead, it is on looking at all sides of the dispute and considering all alternatives for a solution.

Getting to the Root of a Conflict

Often what people argue about is not *really* what they are arguing about. A friend might blow up because her locker partner's books tumbled out onto the floor when she opened the door. On a different day, she might have laughed at the mess. But because she did not get enough sleep the night before and has a huge test in an hour, the heap of books is no laughing matter.

A student might get furious with his girlfriend for canceling their date. But he might actually be worried about being chosen for the basketball team and just be transferring that anxiety onto his girlfriend. It is impossible to solve a conflict without understanding the real reason for the problem.

Feeling caught in a rut with arguments is often a sign that people are paying too much attention to the wrong things, or not understanding what the fights are really about. For example, battles between teens and their parents that seem to center on friends or curfews are often reflections of much deeper issues, such as privacy and trust.[4]

It can be helpful to try to look at the situation from the other person's viewpoint. This is difficult to do in the heat of an argument, but it can be done a few hours or days later. Sometimes looking at a problem from someone else's perspective helps people understand the issues better. They may be completely different issues than those that were shouted about earlier.

Using an Ear Instead of a Mouth: Why Listening Is an Essential Step

An old Hebrew saying is "The beginning of wisdom is silence."

When working on conflict resolution, it is important to remember that no one will ever understand the opposite point of view until he or she stops talking and starts listening.

It is easy during an argument to be so busy stating one side of the conflict that no one stops to hear the other side. Sometimes, with careful listening, people discover there is more agreement than disagreement.

Getting to the Root of an Argument

- Determine what you are really fighting about. You probably cannot do this in the middle of an argument, but can probably do so later. Talk to friends and see if they can give a fresh perspective. Often if teens are having repeated arguments with their parents, a teacher, or a certain friend, there is an underlying reason for the fights. It may be that a teenager is frustrated that his parents do not trust him, that his teacher's expectations are too high, or that his friends are too critical of his clothing.

- Make a list of what you are fighting about and look for patterns. The argument may start out over a clothing allowance, but the real issue is making purchases without needing to get a parent's permission.

- Ask yourself if you are giving mixed messages. Are you telling your friends that you want to be included in their activities but are always rejecting their invitations? Are you telling your boyfriend you want to break up with him, but you are still spending hours on the phone with him each night? Make sure you are giving out clear information.

There are different ways to listen. Everyone has had the experience of talking to a parent or a friend and realizing that person has his or her mind someplace else and is not really hearing what is being said. In our fast-paced society with televisions and radios competing for conversation,

Looking at a problem from someone else's perspective is an important step in finding a solution.

people often forget to stop and carefully listen to what is being said.

Active listening is a style of listening in which people are actually hearing and understanding what is said.

Linda Lantieri and Janet Patti, the authors of the conflict resolution book, *Waging Peace in Our Schools*, write, "Active listening is really listening with the heart. It helps us defuse anger and hostility and gain information."[5]

Sometimes people think listening is what happens when they take a breath and wait to make their next statement. But it is much more than that. Active listening—an essential communications tool—involves setting everything aside and truly paying attention to the person who is speaking.

When people are actively listening, they are not also thinking about the football game on Friday or the report that is due tomorrow. Instead, they are giving all of their attention to the person who is speaking.

People who are active listeners are better able to understand the other person's feelings and learn his or her perspective. Active listening techniques include:

Paraphrasing is when someone repeats the information he or she has just heard, but rewords it a bit. It can feel artificial at first, but it is a good way to make sure a person is hearing the right information.

"I am hearing you say that when I take the car without permission, you feel like I am not showing you respect."

Clarification is a way of getting more understanding and information by asking some additional questions.

"What did you mean when you said that?" "When did this begin?" or "How did you feel about it?"

Reflection is similar to paraphrasing but it focuses on the underlying feelings someone might have. It is a way to echo back the feelings you may hear from someone.

"You sound really sad about that." Be aware that at times we misjudge someone's feelings, so this also can be a time for that person to correct us and say, "No, I'm not sad, I'm angry."

Encouraging is a way of getting people to continue talking.

"Go ahead and tell me about it. I want to hear what you have to say."

Validation is a step in active listening that can be effective because it lets the person know their sharing information is appreciated.

"I know you are uncomfortable, but I'm glad you are telling me about this."

Summarizing is when someone briefly recaps what the other person said. The summary is a shortened version of what was said.

"So my understanding is that you still want to be friends if I stop gossiping about you."

Working Toward New Solutions

Knowing the difference between arguing and conflict resolution helps teens understand whether they are focused on problem solving or making the problems worse. Getting to the root of a dispute by clearly understanding what people are in disagreement about is necessary before people can begin looking for solutions. And active listening is needed throughout the process as a way to make sure everyone is being heard and being heard accurately.

4

Fight or Flight?
Finding a
Middle Ground

Peacemaking is not easy. In many ways, it is much more difficult than making war. But its great rewards cannot be measured in ordinary terms.

—Former President Jimmy Carter[1]

Some people think resolving conflict means giving in and giving up. It is easy enough to resolve a conflict with a friend about which movie to see by agreeing to go to the one he chose. And there is nothing wrong with making compromises. But a steady diet of giving in is not a healthy solution.

Broccoli is nutritious and tasty. But eating nothing but broccoli would make anyone sick. Conflict resolution is similar. If someone settled every conflict by giving in to what his friend wanted, he probably would end up feeling put down or angry. If someone settled every conflict by insisting on winning, he probably would not have very many friends. So a balance must be found in conflict resolution.

The Chinese symbol for crisis is formed by combining the symbols for both danger and opportunity.[2] Maybe a similar symbol is needed for conflict and conflict resolution. Conflict can create both danger and opportunity.

All teens deal with conflict differently. Some seem to bristle at the slightest problem and appear eager for a fight. Others walk away from any dispute and are fearful about disagreeing with people.

Most teens are somewhere in the middle. They may get angry and argue about issues that are truly important to them. But they will also let the small stuff go.

People learn how to respond to conflict when they are children. If they grew up in a family that regularly disagrees without any major explosions, they may learn that disagreements are not threatening.[3] But if they grew up in a home with fighting, name-calling, and threats—disagreements can be overwhelming. They might have an exaggerated response to slight conflicts and either become panicked or get aggressive.[4]

Teens learn coping strategies for dealing with conflict. Sometimes what they have learned as children will serve them well. But other times, it can work against them because they see danger where there is none.

Fight or Flight?

Justin was familiar with fights, although he rarely threw a punch. Smaller than most teens his age, Justin had numerous health problems. In grade school, playground bullies regularly targeted him for abuse. Several times, he came home with broken glasses and bruises. Justin's grade school survival strategy was to allow the bullies to hit him and attempt to escape as quickly as possible. He never reported them and he never fought back.

That may have worked for him in grade school, but Justin's style of handling conflict was not working well in middle school. There he applied the same approach to classroom disagreements, only instead of getting physical, he simply always let the other students win the arguments and kept his opinions to himself. His teacher gave him a bad grade for not participating, and he regularly felt frustrated.

Shawna was a wild kid. Her grade school principal knew her well from her regular trips to his office after playground scuffles. The youngest of four children, Shawna had learned to be aggressive just to keep from being overwhelmed by her older siblings. Now as a teenager, her aggressive style was costing her friends. She had a reputation of arguing to win every disagreement, no matter how small. Although she set aside her physical fighting, her words packed a solid punch. She is not sure why she has so few friends.

Justin and Shawna are stuck using conflict styles that may have worked for them as children but certainly are not working as teens. Luckily, anyone can learn conflict resolution skills and use them in daily life. It just takes practice and a bit of discovery about each teen's conflict style.

Learning a New Approach

People's responses to conflict can be categorized into three basic groups: soft, hard, and principled responses. Most people use all three approaches at different times.[5]

In both soft and hard responses, the people arguing take positions or stands relative to the problem. They then negotiate these positions by trying either to avoid or to win a contest of wills.

Soft and hard negotiations either bring about one-sided losses or demand one-sided gains. In principled responses, the people use conflict resolution strategies to produce lasting "wise agreements" that deal with the interests of both people, resolve conflicting interests fairly, and take into account how others will be affected by the agreement.

One of the first steps in finding a good way to deal with conflicts is for teens to identify what they do now. By reading these descriptions of a typical daily conflict, teens can find the response they would be most likely to use.

Sharon and Tami are ninth graders who have been best friends since kindergarten. They share everything: clothes, makeup, and secrets. Last weekend, Tami borrowed Sharon's favorite pair of jeans to wear rollerblading. When Tami fell off a curb, she tore a huge hole in the jeans. Sharon, who was going to wear the jeans for a date this weekend, is about to get the news.

Look at the different responses Sharon could have depending upon her conflict resolution style.

Soft Conflict Resolution Response

Tami: "I am so sorry. I can't believe I ruined your favorite jeans. I don't know what to do."

Sharon: "It is ok. I didn't really like them that much. I'm just glad you didn't get hurt."

Tami: "Do you want me to pay for them or give you a pair of mine?"

Sharon: "No, it's fine. Really, it doesn't matter. I didn't want to wear them anymore, anyway."

Soft responses such as avoidance, accommodation, and compromise usually occur between people who are friends or who want to be pleasant to each other because they will continue to have contact in the future.

Some teens using a soft response might try to avoid conflict altogether by withdrawing from the situation, ignoring it, or denying that the conflict even matters.

Accommodation is when one person gives in to the position of the other without seeking to serve his or her own interests. Compromise is when the people arguing agree to something that does not really address the interests of either one but does end the argument.

While a soft response might work well in some situations, it can be a problem if it is a teen's *only* approach to conflict. Constantly using a soft response can leave a teen feeling disillusioned, anxious, or fearful. People who always give in rarely get what they want. In time, they may resent their friends because teens who only use a soft response are not being honest with others about what they need or want. Their opinions and ideas get lost in the constant compromise.

Hard Conflict Resolution Response

Take another look at Tami and Sharon and see what might happen if Sharon took a hard response to the news about her torn jeans.

> *Tami*: "I am so sorry. I can't believe I ruined your favorite jeans. I don't know what to do."

> *Sharon*: "I can't believe you ruined them! You knew they were my favorite jeans. You always do this. You have to buy me an identical pair and I need them tonight."

> *Tami*: "But I won't have any money until I baby-sit on Saturday, and even then I don't know if I'll have

enough. I can probably get you another pair in a week and you could borrow anything of mine until then."

Sharon: "I don't want to wear your clothes. I want you to get me a new pair of jeans just like the ones you borrowed. How you come up with the money is your problem."

Tami: "I guess I'll find some way to get them."

Usually hard responses to conflict happen between people who are adversaries and whose goal is victory. On the sports field, this type of response can win an athletic scholarship. But in relationships, it can cause big problems.

Hard responses to a conflict can include force, threats, aggression, and anger. Hard negotiators demand concessions as a condition of the relationship and insist on their position. They often search for a single answer to the problem—usually the one that lets them win.

Hard negotiators frequently apply pressure, trying to win a contest of wills. They use bribery and punishments such as withholding money, favors, and affection. Hard responses hurt relationships and can result in hostility, physical damage, and violence.

Principled Conflict Resolution Response

Notice that by using a principled conflict resolution response, Tami and Sharon are able to find a solution that works and neither one is hiding her feelings about the disagreement.

Tami: "I am so sorry. I can't believe I ruined your favorite jeans. I don't know what to do."

Sharon: "I'm really disappointed that you tore them. I really like them and I wanted to wear them this weekend. Now I'm stuck."

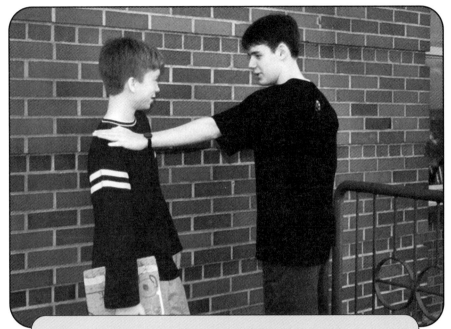

Some teens mistakenly think that fighting is an ideal way of resolving conflicts.

Tami: "I could lend you a pair of my jeans."

Sharon: "That would help, but I think you should replace the pair you tore."

Tami: "I wish I could, but I don't have enough money. It might take a couple of weeks to earn it."

Sharon: "I do want you to replace the jeans and if it takes a few weeks, that's ok."

People who are problem solvers usually pick a principled response to conflict. They have a goal of finding an outcome that works for both people without a fight. Communication is essential to finding a principled solution and often this approach is not as fast as the others.

What Is Your Style?

- Do you always like to win arguments? Are you more concerned with winning an argument than with hearing the reasons for the other person's opinion? You are using a hard response.

- Do you constantly give in? Are you more concerned about not hurting anyone's feelings or inconveniencing anyone than you are about getting what you want? You are using a soft response.

- Are you able to slow down and listen to both sides of a disagreement? Are you able to tell people what you want and hear what they want? Do you look for a win-win solution? Congratulations, you are using a principled response.

Now, take a few minutes and, on a separate piece of paper, write down a short description of the last few conflicts you had. Maybe they were with your parents, your teachers, your siblings, or your friends.

- What was the argument about?
- What did you want? What did the other person want?
- Do you know why they wanted that?
- How did you resolve the conflict?
- How did you feel afterward?
- Was there a possible solution that could have worked for everyone?
- What might you do differently next time?

If people work together instead of fighting, they are more likely to come up with a win-win solution than an angry standoff.

Using a principled response to conflict preserves relationships. If people work toward a principled response, they are likely to find more cooperation in places where they once found conflict. That is because this response does not create a winner and a loser. Instead people work together to find a solution.

5

Roadblocks to Success

You can't shake hands with a clenched fist.

—Indira Gandhi [1]

Erika felt as if she were living in a war zone. Every day she and her mom found something new to fight about. When Erika got dressed, her mom told her that her shirt was too tight and she needed to wear a sweatshirt. When she had a friend over to talk, her mom said she was wasting time, and when she did not invite a friend over, her mom said she was being a loner. Erika felt like it was even worse at home now that her mom had remarried. Nothing was going right. Usually they would end up shouting at each other and saying things they both regretted.

Erika felt more comfortable with her dad. He lived just a few minutes away and she visited him every other weekend and one night a week. Her dad was just as strict as her mom was, but he and Erika got along better. Erika really wanted to live with him and just visit her mom. But she was afraid to say anything to either parent because she did not want to start an argument.

Erika had been learning about conflict resolution at school, yet she had not really tried the techniques. They felt awkward and she was not sure she could maintain her cool while disagreeing with her parents. Usually she ended up shouting, and once she even got into a shoving match with her mom. But she wanted to try something different.

She decided she would state her problem directly, without complaining, and would share her solution. She would explain why she believed it would work. And if they objected to her idea, she was determined to listen to their ideas and not lose her cool. She even wrote down her ideas to help stay on track.[2]

Making Changes Can Be Confusing for Everyone

Erika appears to be positioned for success. She has prepared her ideas and she is determined to use her conflict resolution skills. But she might still have problems. Here are a few things people need to consider when they get ready to try new techniques on old problems.

Remember to Listen

Erika is certain she has a good solution for her problem of fighting with her mom. And she is right that it is better to stay calm and not accuse her mom of anything. But she needs to remember to also listen to her parents' ideas and perspectives. By using active listening, she can remain open to solutions they may have. Perhaps her mom and stepdad will not support her moving out, but would support

It can seem as if teens and parents are always in conflict, but peaceful ways can be found to work out disagreements.

her visiting her dad more frequently. Part of conflict resolution includes listening.

Everyone Does Not Have New Tools

It is great that Erika learned new ways to deal with an ongoing problem at home. Unfortunately her whole family was not in the same conflict resolution class, so they may not have the same new tools. Also Erika's past behavior has trained her parents to engage in shouting matches with her. They might start arguing because that is how they have responded in the past.

Seattle therapist Joan Casey encourages people to give family and friends a warning when they are going to try new ways of responding to old problems. She suggests that people share their new tools and their new plan of response ahead of time.[3]

Perhaps Erika should first tell her parents that she wants to work with them on solving problems instead of fighting. It is a good idea for her to share any conflict resolution information she has with them. They are more likely to take her changes more seriously as they see her using the new approach with her friends and siblings.

Change Feels Strange

Once Erika starts using her new conflict resolution skills at home, at school, and with friends, it is likely she will feel awkward and uncomfortable at first. Casey said that when someone changes how he deals with other people, it will feel strange and forced at first. It is like learning any other new skill. The first few times teens try it, they might stumble and feel strange.

Erika found that she felt strange when she did not launch into an argument with her mom. It was hard to stay calm. But she noticed that when she stayed calm, her mom did not yell as much. She told her mom about her new problem-solving plan in a letter and asked her mom to respond the next day.

"I tell my clients that it is a good sign to feel uncomfortable because it means they are trying something new," Casey said. "Just fake it until you make it."[4]

Eventually it will feel normal to work toward solutions instead of staying stuck in arguments with no end.

Erika's mom read her letter and considered her idea about moving in with her dad. But at that point, her mom decided it was better for her and Erika to start working together on fighting less and listening more. Although Erika did not get to move out, she is seeing some improvements in how she and her mom communicate.

Is There Always a Win-Win Solution?

If one friend wants to go to a movie and the other friend wants to go to a concert, is there a solution that will make them both happy? Sometimes there is and sometimes there is not. Occasionally, people will experience a problem where there is no easy answer or where the people remain locked in the conflict. In chess, this is called a stalemate and the game ends. But in life, it continues. So what can people do during a stalemate?

A lot, according to Drs. Jeffrey Rubin and Carol Rubin in their book, *When Families Fight*. Here are some of their suggestions for unlocking a conflict stalemate:

Work Together: Do not give up on the process. Instead, look for ways to help people change their position or expand their options without feeling like they have "given in." It can be very helpful to be the first person to compromise.

Negotiate: "You give this and I'll give that." This approach can include adding new options to be considered or agreeing to give in this time in exchange for getting your way next time.

Communicate: Make an honest effort to view the problem from the other person's perspective. Practice active listening to see if there is a hidden problem that is making it harder to find a solution.

Usually there is a way to break a stalemate during a conflict. Sometimes people need to take a break from the conflict for a few hours or days and try to find a solution when they are rested or less angry.[5]

Moving Beyond the Disagreement to Reconciliation

Once people have found a solution to their conflict, they need to let go of the disagreement and move forward. Often they also need to rebuild the friendship or relationship. This is called reconciliation, a time when people who have been in a disagreement come together again after reaching a solution. Sometimes it can be hard to do this, especially if people became angry or emotional during the conflict resolution process.

For the reconciliation to be successful, everyone must be able to establish a vision for the future that lets go of blame, punishment, and damages and that recognizes each person's value.[6] Usually for this to happen, the people involved need to feel as if they are comfortable with the agreement and that their concerns were heard. If people think the settlement was unfair, they cannot move on to reconciliation because they are holding onto resentment or anger.

6

Using Conflict Resolution Skills in the Community

The vast majority of young people do not carry weapons, do not deal drugs, do not join gangs and do not victimize their friends or neighborhoods. Most young people, like most adults, want nothing more than to lead their lives in peace.

—pamphlet from Harborview Hospital (Seattle, Washington) Injury Prevention Researchers[1]

Peacemaking Happens Every Day

Peacemaking and conflict resolution efforts do not usually get the same headlines as wars, shootings, and even shouting matches between well-known people.

It is rare to see lead television news stories about the people who sit around tables trying to find a compromise that might end a war. Equally rare is any mention of the many teens who work at helping their peers settle disagreements peacefully.

The news media is a lot like the school lunchroom. Not many students sit at lunch and whisper about which teens settled their disagreements peacefully. They are more likely to talk about the few teens who threatened to fight it out. The same is true in the news. Reporters rarely tell about the airplanes that landed safely each day. Instead, they tell of the few crashes.

But each day most teens settle their disagreements without a fight.

While they do not get a lot of publicity, peacemaking and conflict resolution efforts are rapidly growing.

In 1999, President Bill Clinton launched a federal program to offer more than $100 million in grants to fifty-four

Although they do not get a lot of publicity, conflict resolution efforts are rapidly growing.

cities. These grants were to make schools safer and to help keep young people safe from aggressive behavior. Many of these programs include conflict resolution techniques. President Clinton also said some of the money would be used to hire 147 more school resource officers.[2] These resource officers are police officers in the school. But their role is much broader than the typical law enforcement found in other police work. They teach students about the dangers of abusing drugs and alcohol as well as about the benefits of being nonviolent.

"We need to nurture the personal strengths of children and adolescents so they can resolve problems without resorting to violence, alcohol, drugs and suicide," said Donna Shalala, U.S. Secretary of Health and Human Services.[3]

Peer Mediation Programs

At Fairhaven Middle School in Bellingham, Washington, counselor Marilyn McClellan opens a three-ring binder to review the results of the peer mediation efforts. Her school has nearly one peer mediation each day. Peer mediation teaches teens to help other students resolve their disagreements fairly and peacefully.[4]

More than ten thousand schools nationwide now offer peer mediation.[5] Each program is slightly different. The programs usually involve training a group of students to remain neutral. This means they do not take sides in other people's arguments. Peer mediators are also taught to let the people in conflict come up with solutions. Usually peer mediation programs are designed to reach a consensus (an agreement), maintain confidentiality (mediators should not discuss what happened in mediation with other students), and avoid blame.

Peer mediation follows this six-step process:

- *Set the stage.*

  The peer mediator brings the teens in conflict together to work on their problem. Usually only teens who are willing to work on a solution go to peer mediation. The process requires willing participation.

- *Gather perspectives.*

  The mediator invites each person in conflict to describe the problem. Active listening is used to make sure the person is heard correctly. No interrupting or debating is allowed.

- *Identify interests.*

  The peer mediator works with the people in conflict to make sure everyone understands what is at the root of their conflict. They also learn what each person feels is at stake in finding a solution.

- *Create options.*

  The teens in conflict are encouraged to brainstorm every possible solution to the conflict. During brainstorming, every idea is welcomed and no ideas are criticized.

- *Evaluate options.*

  The mediator helps the people in conflict sort through the possible solutions to see if they can find a solution that is acceptable for everyone.

- *Generate agreement.*

  Once a solution is found, the peer mediator writes a short contract stating the agreement. The people in conflict sign the agreement.

One study of a peer mediation program in a suburban high school found that students who were sent to peer mediation were less likely to be referred back to the vice principal within the following two and one-half months than those who were given traditional discipline.[6]

The notebook at Fairhaven Middle School lists the areas of disagreement and the solutions that were reached in the peer mediations. They include teens arguing about name-calling, rumor spreading, minor threats, minor fighting, and the theft of schoolwork. The solutions include apologies, repayment or replacement of damaged things, and deciding to stay apart for a while.

"We do not send major problems like sexual harassment, violence or drug and alcohol issues into peer mediation,"

Peer mediation groups can be extremely helpful in allowing teens to discuss conflicts in a calm and organized manner.

McClellan said. "Those issues still are primarily dealt with by adults."

Teen mediators also are taught to end the mediation if any student loses his temper, becomes threatening, or refuses to help find a solution, McClellan said.

Taking Conflict Resolution Skills to the Community

Teens in school now are part of the first generation of students who have been taught widespread conflict resolution and anger management skills.

"I think teens have wonderful skills these days," McClellan said. "I believe these skills will impact their lives."

Students at her school are bringing back success stories of settling conflicts with their parents and friends by working toward solutions together. And some students are taking their skills beyond their personal relationships.[7]

A Harris survey in the late 1990s showed that nine out of ten teens said they would be willing to take an active role in trying to do something about violence through mentoring, education, or community awareness programs.[8]

Increasingly, mediation is being required in divorces that include children. Some states require divorcing parents to settle custody issues through mediation instead of court battles.

Students who were successful peer mediators in middle school are sometimes being asked to help with custody mediation at professional mediation sites. McClellan said she has been asked to recommend older students to work in such cases, especially those involving custody of teenagers.

"Some of these teens are very talented mediators who will be a great asset to the community," she said.[9]

Appendix

Anger Is an Emotion, Violence Is a Choice

Feel Your Anger Signs

You can feel the changes in your body when you get angry. Use these as your warning signs telling you to take action to calm down.

When you are angry you may feel:

- Muscle tension, especially in your neck and shoulders
- Accelerated heartbeat: Your heart feels like it is racing
- A knot or butterflies in your stomach
- Changes in your breathing. You might feel like you cannot take a deep breath
- Trembling, almost as if you were too cold
- Goose bumps on your skin
- Flushed in the face. You face may look as if you are blushing. Your cheeks may feel hot

Learn How to Calm Down

You can reduce the rush of adrenaline that is causing the feelings you experience when your anger starts to boil over.

- Take a few slow, deep breaths and concentrate on slowing your breathing.
- Imagine yourself someplace where you usually feel calm: in your bedroom, in the forest, at a beach.

- Keep telling yourself: I do not need to prove myself. I can calm down. I am not going to let him or her get to me.

Consider the Consequences

- Try to think of a positive or neutral reason for what the person did.
- Do not argue in front of other people.
- Make your goal to defeat the problem, not the person.
- Recognize what sets you off and how the anger feels.
- Stay calm and think about your actions.

Based upon: "Warning Signs" American Psychological Association Brochure produced with MTV Networks. For free copies of the complete brochure, call (800) 268-0078.

Four Steps for Turning a Conflict into Consensus

1. Separate the people from the problem

Every disagreement or problem has real issues and issues that deal more with the personalities of the people involved. If you can focus on the real problem, not the people, you can all work together to find a solution.

If people are feeling too emotional, take a break to give everyone a chance to calm down or blow off steam before you work on finding a solution.

2. Focus on interests, not positions

Interests define the problem. Positions are something a person decides he wants. Make sure you get to the root of people's interests. These might not be easy to see at first.

3. Create options that let both parties or people gain something

Brainstorm many options, even ones that are not your first choice. Remember while you are brainstorming you should not criticize or evaluate the ideas. That comes later.

4. Use a fair way to choose between the solutions

Neither person should feel as if he lost or won.

Source: Principles of Conflict Resolution, National Center for Conflict Resolution Education, <http://www.nccre.org/guide/principles.html> (March 5, 2000).

Chapter Notes

Chapter 1. Finding Solutions Without Giving Up or Giving In

1. Kofi Annan, secretary general of the United Nations, Hague Appeal for Peace Conference Page, 1999, <http://www.haguepeace.org> (February 22, 2000).

2. Centers for Disease Control, "Facts About Violence Among Youth and Violence in Schools," federal Center for Disease Control page on School Violence, n.d., <http://www.cdc.gov/ncipc/factsheets/schoolvi.htm> (February 22, 2000).

3. K. Dwyer, D. Osher, and C.Warger, "Early Warning, Timely Response: A Guide to Safe Schools," United States Department of Education, 1998, <http://www.ed/gov/offices/OSERS/OSEP/earlywrn.html> (March 12, 2000).

4. Centers for Disease Control.

5. "What They Said," news staff, *The* (Eugene, Ore.) *Register Guard*, May 22, 1998, A-5, Thurston Tragedy page, <http://www.registerguard.com> (February 22, 2000).

6. Linda Lantieri and Janet Patti, *Waging Peace in Our Schools* (Boston: Beacon Press, 1996), p. 19.

7. The Carter Center, Peace Programs Page, n.d., <http://www.cartercenter.org> (February 22, 2000).

8. Lantieri, p. 19.

Chapter 2. Teenagers Have a Steady Diet of Conflict

1. Personal interview with Brittany, January 2000. (Real name withheld to protect privacy.)

2. Robert Berkow, *The Merck Manual of Medical Information* (Rahway, N.J.: Merck, Sharp & Dohme Research Laboratories, 1997), p. 1255.

3. Lawrence Kutner, Ph.D., *Making Sense of Your Teenager* (New York: William Morrow, 1997), p. 26.

4. Ibid., p. 27.

5. Barbara Williams Cosentino, R.N, CSW, "It's a Mad, Mad World," *Ten to Eighteen: Parenting Through the Teen Years*, August 1999, vol. 2, no. 6, p.10.

Chapter 3. Being Powerful Without Fighting

1. Harry Esteve, "Clinton Listens, Consoles," *The* (Eugene, Ore.) *Register Guard*, June 14, 1998, A-1.

2. Personal interview with David Shields, January 2000.

3. Institute for Conflict Analysis and Resolution page, George Mason University, n.d., <http://www.gmu.edu/departments/ICAR/index.html> (February 22, 2000).

4. Lawrence Kutner, Ph.D., *Making Sense of Your Teenager* (New York: William Morrow, 1997), pp. 28–29.

5. Linda Lantieri and Janet Patti, *Waging Peace in Our Schools* (Boston: Beacon Press, 1996), pp. 67–74.

Chapter 4. Fight or Flight? Finding a Middle Ground

1. Jimmy Carter, *Talking Peace: A Vision for the Next Generation* (New York: Dutton Children's Books, 1993), p. xiv.

2. Linda Lantieri and Janet Patti, *Waging Peace in Our Schools* (Boston: Beacon Press, 1996), p. 53.

3. Ibid., pp. 52–54.

4. Karen L. Kinnear, *Violent Children* (Santa Barbara, Calif.: ABC-CLIO, Inc., 1995), pp. 14–32.

5. Adapted from: Donna Crawford, and Richard Bodine, *A Guide to Implementing Programs in Schools, Youth-Serving Organizations, and Community and Juvenile Justice Settings*, Office of Juvenile Justice and Delinquency Prevention, U.S. Department of Justice, October 1996.

Chapter 5. Roadblocks to Success

1. Justin Kaplan, ed., *Bartlett's Familiar Quotations* (Boston: Little, Brown & Company, 1992), p. 52.

2. Personal interview with Erika, January 2000. (Real name withheld to protect privacy.)

3. Personal interview with Joan Casey, M.S.W., September 10, 1999.

4. Personal interview with Casey.

5. Dr. Jeffrey Rubin and Dr. Carol Rubin, *When Families Fight: How to Handle Conflict With Those You Love* (New York: William Morrow, 1989), pp. 61–74.

6. Stewart Levine, *Getting to Resolution: Turning Conflict Into Collaboration* (San Francisco: Berrett-Koehler Publishers, Inc., 1998), pp. 4–10.

Chapter 6. Using Conflict Resolution Skills in the Community

1. "Youth Violence: Scope of the Problem," Harborview Injury Prevention and Research Center, University of Washington, July 20, 1997, <http://depts.washington.edu/hiprc/childinjury/topic/violence> (February 17, 2000).

2. Ibid.

3. United States Department of Justice press release, September 11, 1999, <http://www.ed.gov/offices/OESE/SDFS> (March 12, 2000).

4. Personal interview with school counselor Marilyn McClellan, February 29, 2000.

5. Kathiann Kowalski, "Peer Mediation Success Stories," *Current Health 2*, October 1998, vol. 25, no. 2, p. 13.

6. "Youth Violence Interventions: Peer Mediation," Harborview Injury Prevention and Research Center, University of Washington, July 20, 1997, <http://depts.washington.edu/hiprc/childinjury/topic/violence> (February 17, 2000).

7. Personal interview with McClellan.

8. "When Violence Comes to School," *Current Health 2*, April–May 1998, vol. 24, no. 8, p. 6.

9. Personal interview with McClellan.

Further Reading

Books

Bell, Ruth. *Changing Bodies, Changing Lives*. New York: Random House, 1998.

Graham Scott, Gini, Ph.D. *Resolving Conflict with Others and Within Yourself*. Oakland, Calif.: New Harbinger Publications, Inc., 1990.

Kinnear, Karen L. *Violent Children*. Santa Barbara, Calif.: ABC-CLIO, 1995.

Lickson, Charles P. *Ironing It Out: Seven Simple Steps to Resolving Conflict*. Menlow Park, Calif.: Crisp Publishers, 1996.

MacBeth, Fiona. *Playing with Fire: Creative Conflict Resolution for Young Adults*. Gabriola Island, British Columbia, Canada: New Society Publishing, 1995.

Ury, William L. *Getting to Peace: Transforming Conflict at Home, at Work & in the World*. New York: Viking Press, 1999.

Weeks, Dudley, Ph.D. *The Eight Essential Steps to Conflict Resolution*. Los Angeles: Jeremy P. Tarcher, Inc., 1994.

Pamphlets

Love Doesn't Have to Hurt Teens. American Psychological Association, 1997.

Sheley, Joseph F. and James D. Wright. *High School Youths, Weapons, and Violence: A National Survey*. Research in Brief, October 1998.

Internet Sites

National Crime Prevention Council

This organization has many resources for the prevention of crime and violence.

> 1700 K Street NW
> Washington, D.C. 20006–3817
> (202) 466-6272
> <http://www.weprevent.org>

Center to Prevent Handgun Violence

This organization works for better laws and enforcement of existing laws that promote gun control, handgun safety, and the prevention of handgun violence.

> 1225 Eye Street, NW, Suite 1100
> Washington, D.C. 20005
> (202) 898-0792
> <http://www.handguncontrol.org>

Educators for Social Responsibility

This organization promotes the teaching of social responsibility in all levels of schools. It focuses on peacemaking and conflict resolution programs.

> Resolving Conflict Creatively Program
> Educators for Social Responsibility
> 40 Exchange Place, Suite 1111
> New York, NY 10005
> (212) 509-0022
> <http://www.esrnational.org>

Students Against Violence Everywhere

This organization is for students who are actively working to promote nonviolent solutions to problems in their schools, community, and country. It was created by Mothers Against Violence In America *organization.*

(800) 897-7697
<http://www.mavia.org/save.htm>

PeaceBuilders

This program promotes long-term, community-based violence reduction and crime prevention through school and community programs.

(877) 4 -Peacenow
<http://www.peacebuilders.com>

National Center for Conflict Resolution Education

This federally sponsored center collects information about many different types of conflict resolution programs. It includes contact information and studies about the effectiveness of these programs.

Illinois Bar Center
424 S. Second Street
Springfield, IL 62701
<http://www.nccre.org>

United Nations Cyber School Bus

The United Nations operates this Web site, which provides information on UN peacekeeping, poverty, and global teaching projects.

Cyber School Bus
One United Nations Plaza
RM DC1-552
New York, NY 10017
(212) 963-8589
<http://www.un.org/Pubs/CyberSchoolBus>

Index